Nihilistic City Nights

Robert Yates

William Cornelius Harris Publishing

In collaboration

With

London Poetry Books

ISBN 978-1-911232-11-7

20 Spendlow Drive ME5 9JT

London Poetry Books

London Poetry Books

Contents

Nihilistic City Night

these are the orange-strobed hours
of insomnia
and blinding glass
when visionaries pound against walls
and streets melt into 1980s parody

neighbours' stereos deny all literature
(there is no room for thought)

the sky is drawn down in racist screams,
entangled by fireworks

and now the strength to dream
is robbed and infected

and called unprintable names

Happy New Year

the beautiful, uninviting
abodes of victory

loom above the circuit to my flat

and I, who am yet to perfect
the art of cruelty,

am tamed and disinspired by that

Rorschach's Face

he lives his own 1985, hidden
from the sunlight
of Boris Becker and Live Aid

his protean mask is that of
victims, failures, school inmates

he turns his face from management
requirements and strives to mould
the storming present into eternity
(he also beats up petty criminals)

careers advisers and doctors see in him
inappropriate affect
or maybe he's just lazy

disintegrating space shuttles mean even less to him
than time-travelling DeLoreans

miners' strikes and nuclear meltdowns
pass over him like Saint Elmo's fire

he sees the truth in mutable realities, exploding clocks
and the death of comedians

Last night I dreamt of Allison Scagliotti

I had no lines; I felt as futile
as Philip K Dick, droning on about his 1974 epiphany
(religion got him in the end
religion and all those drugs)

last night I dreamt of Allison Scagliotti
"don't go to her gig," they warned me
"she'll probably do a Pixies cover"

I fast-forwarded through the boring bits in Warehouse 13
and, as you can imagine, they were many

I bumped into a bright young thing
who had once lived inside Brideshead Revisited
"It is far too hot today, Yates"
"Sorry, madam"
"And what have you been up to?"
"Well, last night I dreamt
of Allison Scagliotti," I replied, reaching for a handy can of Ubik

there was something about Claudia's knowing smile and
ironic references to her psychiatric past
I was comforted by biography

Twelve second instrumental

living without your love is like a 12 second instrumental
where all the myths of relationships coincide

you become your image

don't deprive yourself of being mournful
your experience could overthrow ideologies

as clouds in their gathering might
never terminating quite
the purple shoulder arched at night

City Piece

"Voici le soir charmant, ami du criminel" Baudelaire

Borne on the dusk, our feet trip over the pair of frozen phoenixes on top of the Liver Building. There is something in the air: the grey outline of expectancy.

On the ground, we are assaulted by language. The bus stops are moved and the trains go where they will (change at a shimmering recollection of industrial revolutions). Nothing you conjure or describe will help you in the struggle towards existence; in Carl Jung's dream Liverpool is the pool of life.

I could resurrect the mornings of brutality – the uncapturable images – for you to play with them.

Far to the east, a magical storm cloud roils above the walls of Pavis and an occult murmur insinuates itself through the streets of Arkham.

Notes

The quote from Baudelaire I would translate as "Here comes the beguiling evening, the criminal's friend". I refer to three imaginary cities: Pavis, Arkham and Liverpool. Pavis is a fantasy city created by Greg Stafford in the 1970s. Arkham is a fictional city created by H. P. Lovecraft in 1920. Liverpool is a shared hallucination. According to an urban legend, the birds on the Liver Building are not swans or cormorants, as was traditionally believed, but are a mythical species of bird peculiar to Liverpool. There are two birds, a female and a male: the female looks out at sea to see when the ships come in; the male looks inland to the city to find out what time the pubs open.

The Sea

sea, when in the morning of imprisonment
your clouds broke through school windows

washing over coastal towns
where worlds are created
on rainy afternoons

sparkling like night memory

in distant cities bohemians
reinvent the shameful past
in which there never was a sea

Failed scenes

I cannot contain the intensity that unfolds before me.
Cézanne

Daylight was failing and so were the two unpublished writers
witnessing its demise. One of them, half-hidden by a curtain, stared out
of the window. "What's that mask he's always wearing?" he demanded,
then, turning into the darkened room, addressed his accomplice:
"Things are going to change. Next year, when I get my licence, I'll be
able to drive anywhere…"

Across town, an immense stinking night settled over the port, muffled
screams rang out against menacing walls and nameless estates, an urban
shaman was threatened for the capital crime of being strange, like in a
Robert E Howard yarn, beautiful exotic cities culminated in sudden
violence, an unending schizophrenic story.

At the collage of further education, a frustrated bow-legged art teacher
waddled apoplectically to class and obedient English Lit students strove
futilely to change the world through language.

Autumn

when the sky overreaches
and the street mirrors
the fullness of ambition

the one night stands eternal

into the light
couples return
far from the horror of burnt-out warehouses
and darkened flats

the rain sparkles with sordid affairs

fumbling out of the detritus of years
to form an incantation

Winter

snapping the ties of human resources
and the mundurbanity of neighbours

I leap at the primordial sky and
feel a neologism coming on

amid the dark branches' trembling
your stretched tights foreshadow
air strikes – crescendos
from the future's ancient languages

that haircut deserved a wider audience

Timescape

The streets were losing touch with reality; they had been appropriated by a consortium of insane archaeologists and drug pushers.

At night, car headlights drifted across the eternal landscape like Anglo-Saxon ghosts. A social historian is pulled up for referring vaguely to "the people". Blue Peter's Sarah Greene in a Victorian corset insinuated the future's ludic delight. Sighing after the lost elegance of ocean liners and zeppelins, a couple of aesthetes ignore the totalitarian poverty and all that deadly tedium.

And I dream of the (un)resurrected night when I stared the dark scintillating city in the face, deciphered its languages, plotted its movements. Neither scousers nor teachers shat upon my literature; and there were no utility bills to bring it down.

Untitled Too

The wings of a stealth fighter dip into the encroaching blackness; a memory of snowed-in night to allay girlfriends and future threats.

An agoraphobic flâneur dons his Gothic best and sets out to stalk the darkened city. A reporter is mugged and robbed of his plans.

In an isolated castle, aristocrats who have chosen to sit out the war are plagued by petty tensions, unspoken passions. At least they look good: baroque statues recalling the dusty and vaguely insalubrious dalliances of alchemists and philosophes.

And on long hot nights streaked with cocaine taken far from any source of inspiration – the scented leaves the holocaust of summer – the debauched promise of a lie in. The city can describe itself.

After a Dream

Liverpool had been shaken by English literature, although we had both been advised to do modern languages with business studies. From the towering remains of the Pantheon to the submerged feet of Abu Simbel, the industrial revolution had shattered all monuments. The air pulsed with imminent creativity.

Trembling for a bus at Saint George's Hall, we would avoid the future's years of cosy nothing: fingers steeple behind cloistered windows analysing political correctness and technique. The D6 takes us through sluggish housing estates into the game. As the dying screams of sunset resounded through darkened streets, the aftermath ruins grumbled contradictory mythologies.

Through sepulchral dawns fallout plastered the faces of untold victims into marble statues; we were forced to hide from the gangs who murdered words with dialects; and wait apprehensively for the punctilious headmistress swishing angrily across the rich carpet of her study.

Movement

arcing off its route, our bus
sparks tangents – dislodges new myths
to the disparagement of teenaged grognards

and the adumbration of
memorials against the paling sky –
in the polluted streaks of sunset
harbour all the frustrations of voyages

stations decay into museums
and the road divides into other possible lives

Let me know when you wake up

your life terrifies me like cocaine
in its strength and subtlety of beauty

i cannot eat
the storm
lacks violence

and nothing really matters but this
rejection of morose reality

unspoken answers, alphabet games
hot wax seals your arms' ellipsis

text me in the morning, saying

Pimlico

under empty sky
the days begin to january

and through cold sunlit streets
a wandering ghost tries to

latch onto lives
those second-hand unread bookshops

future stresses haunt the unused hours

at the edge of the night, erased
messages offer pain and other drugs

Ode to Indifference

indifference! Insensible as lost desire
or evenings when there have been too many songs
reality is bigger – there – unmentioned

in the night's close understood silence
i am a pillow and scrap paper;

this poem wasn't working anyway

Pastoral

Escaping from northern hills whose inhabitants' peculiarities have been unwarped and unstraightened by cities sounds a clarion call and the beagles and hunt saboteurs are misunderstood by locals. The police drive away.

We are not obsessed by music, only multilingual signs, the jealous freedom of weekend drives. If you want to be healthy, go and do it somewhere else.

Once, at twenty, the woodland copse swam in a haze of setting light - but nowadays we stumble back to our bodies in a grey dream of dawn through whose mist rings a church bell and echoes of work.

A landscape of collapsed tents: loneliness and horror. I have gone the way of Scottish film-makers who trade on their accents. Jangling of nerves: toward the still feverish trees stretch out distancing paces – epitaphs for a delusion.

The Haunting

Am i the only homeless person here?

(or like the others ignorant of lovecraft)
do not send me away, because the dead
years are dearer than life

and the faces in the wallpaper
that hides the suicide room
speak louder than any special effect

let me spend the night with your psychoses
laughing as invisible demons pound on the wall

lead me in the dark to the winding stair
that buckles and shakes until i fall
and waits for another, and leads nowhere

Lonely Man's Wine

(after Baudelaire)

A gallant woman's singular glance
Sliding towards us like the white beam
The undulating moon sends to the trembling lake
Where she wishes to bathe her nonchalant beauty;

The last bag of coins in a gamer's hands;
A wanton kiss from some skinny flirt;
Annoying and tender, musical sounds
Like the distant cry of humanity's hurt

None of that equals, bottle deep,
The penetrating balms you keep
For the sacred poet's debased heart

You pour him hope and youth and life
And the beggar's only treasure – pride,
That turns us all conquering, godlike!

Opus 21 (Pretension)

the self-congratulatory imagery of creators
– oh, what shocking nightmares! –
like the faintly ridiculous constructs of masochists

reiterating a tedious trauma
recording without conviction
performance debilitating literature

the cursory suicides accumulate
an apology of attempt

empty phrase

like the sociability of psychopaths
brutality of enthusiasm
in the absence of intoxication

Ode to Uziel Gal

(In ballistics, a choke is the constriction at the end of a shotgun barrel
by which the firing pattern in controlled.)

there's never a submachinegun around
when you need one:
under the creation-sapping heat
no troll god to devour the sun

in the raucous laughter and insipid
nazism of "glorious weather"
techno 3 a.m. insomnia – no
covering for sweaty chest
– where you goin', dolly?
hey, where you
goin', dolly? I'm!
talkin' to you I said
something!

O for a spray
(on full automatic)
explosion of skulls, rupture of atria
the sweet eulogy of agonising shits
choke on a shotgun,
you bastards (yes I know
an Uzi's not a fucking shotgun)

Notes on the architecture of hell

When the Gate first opened between 1980's Liverpool and Second Empire Paris, he was elsewhere.

It shouldn't've surprised him. The old slave-backed port had developed a magical nexus from the decaying docks, riot memories, neoclassical façades, and the girl at the train station.

He learned about it from an erstwhile friend in Bootle, District Hell 20. They had been sitting together in a coffee-smell caff.

"Y'na thi ald games shop?" said Erstwhile.
"You mean Games?"
"That's the one."

Games had stood in the central circle of Liverpool, where library steps burned with sandstone and sulphur and the damned effigies of queer suicides were rained on eternally by hot pigeon shit.

It was dangerous territory, but he found a taxi.
They dipped into the final firepit and came to a halt by the museum, its walls coated in dried uric acid.

Outside the car, the acrid stench of his own armpits made him wince and he found himself accosted by evangelists of the great god Fuck the Omniscient.

"There's a side entrance," they told him. "You can pry back the boards."

He thanked them, gave them the price of an armful of smack, and they reciprocated with their ritual one-fingered salute.

A pigeon fled crackling into the wounded sky.

He crossed to the building which had once housed Games of Liverpool, finding something eerie about the lack of semi-literate graffiti on the window hoardings. Nervously he slouched into a side alley and jemmied up some of the boards.

The dark musty cellar stocked with cobwebbed role-playing games had indeed decayed into a dimensional portal. Maybe that was why the pigeons were so scared. Eliphas Lévi and Joris-Karl Huysmans had certainly done their jobs.

He stepped out of a café on the Boulevard Saint Germain and walked across the deserted Seine. Now he understood how a magical link had developed with late twentieth century Liverpool: the facelifting of Paris under Napoleon the Turd mirrored that of Hell District 1. In neither case had the cosmetic surgery been convincing; cities, he knew, were heavier than stone.

When he returned to Liverpool, it was dusk and the setting sun turned the statue garden into a psychedelic playground.

Trying to find his way to a bus stop, he ran into a twat. It was a Scouse twat and regaled him with theories about the real Liverpool having died and been rebuilt by aliens, who invented The Beatles to keep everyone happy.

He told his new acquaintance to piss off and stop pretending to matter, then cycled away on a tangent.

The Failures

Three ex-friends returned to the city responsible for their condition. In an attempt at emulating the years that had been lived, even then, in the past, they visited their old haunts – as before, without reward.

They drank until maudlin and the barmaid who appeared to be interested in at least one of them, turned out not to be.

And through their conversation it turned out that for all of them life had been a failure.

The first had fallen in love and so had had no success in love. The second had wanted to capture the horror and ecstasy of the city, but they had both escaped. The third had foreseen this reunion many years ago, when they had still been trapped together, and he had done all he could to avoid this ultimate failure. And he had failed.

The ex-friends had grown old and different and the only thing they had in common any more was their frustration.

Yet outside in the city of which they had never really been (a)part, others saw their cherished ambitions annihilated and others, in the moment of victory, carried the memory or threat of defeat.

Fragments

The winter poem went awry. There was something ungraspable about: the expectancy of encroaching nightfall (with flashing images).

Jostled at a burger joint by continentals who knew the word fuck – assumption of common humanity. Like them, I have suffered the inflated transience of urban acquaintance.

Fear of fear of communication; bitterness and silence. I adopt a philosophical attitude to life: Schopenhaueran pessimism.

Why are there always statues of "great people" as if they were a model to which we should aspire, when what society demands is mediocrity? A banal observation in itself.

My employers and neighbours strive to reduce me, to define life by their vexations and prohibit me from saying so.

Interspace

It was surprisingly easy to fall back into the bipolar city, although the spells found in out-of-print role playing games no longer seemed to work. The battle lines were drawn in barbed wire and language – a snippet of a bad song would suffice – for those who had no mouths and had to scream.

Muad'Dib and Maldoror checked that they were being politically correct before catching a bus to the quayside, diverted through the night city towards childhood sand dunes where Colette wrote the only decent novel and got warned that if she continued to waste her time on student demonstrations, she would not be a student any more.

The anaesthetised world rolled in grey banks of cloud muffling thunder. Successful authors well past their prime installed themselves in documentary apartments and failed to write.

Memorial

Night enfolded Liverpool's stifled conflict – lacerating wounds, unable to capture unfolding reality – a bestiality of racisms. When you ran after me towards the station I thought a new time was beginning; and it was, but not the one I imagined. In these hours, sonnets deconstruct, tramp steamers ply the spaces between the stars and prejudices coalesce into theogonies.

We were not playing at being misfits: a misdeclined phrase of Scouse could bring sudden annihilation. We were warned to not be creative. The only appropriate response was silence and parody.

I am petrified by the age of heroines. At the end of the novel, the most moving revelations about our characters' lives are foreshadowed in their early struggles. And the images are eternal.

Notes from a Convention

Ushered out by a fellow conspirator in Victorian dress into the impossibly clear night, which could well last forever, and beckoned far from college windows across lawns and skies to hushed intimations of the king in yellow.

In the morning, the heatwave broke. The fields turned grey as coffee.

End

disintegrating, an alien voice recites my poems
news of publication from a work-shy dawn

i am consigned to the footnotes of your biography,
savour the spittle of open microphones

your amused pierced body lacerates my
panting failure and cowardice

in the nightmare rooms, writers
crumple manuscripts

and in breathless offices
whisper guilty secrets

Profoundly in Love with Pandora

Lou Salomé gives out a tight-laced glare
from the monochrome strictures of her age
wrestling with memories
the eyes that beat Nietzsche

there is something correct about being caned in the snow
exhilarating in the birth of years

and, yes, you shame my existence
in your fierce opening of dreams

once, when I was alive, I reached after mornings, too

The Heaton Generation

this may require a subtlety
that I do not have

to a backdrop of Smiths albums
night blanketed the northern terraces

in songs from the heart of the primal goat
i am avoiding what I really mean

the old buildings of Gray Street
expand into Dostoyevski novels

and the films noirs of the Tyneside
become lost in the heat and chaos of levels

the sudden absence of oppression leaves an aimless abyss
unfillable by language

they will not let me into the poetry reading
because I forgot my prayer mat

Bohemian

A fallen superhero and unfortunate angel were bemused by the city's overdone gigantism.

"If my life falls to pieces," said the angel, "I'll make a fetching dress out of the remains."

As though from his once-accustomed vantage height, the superhero surveyed the tottering ruins of streets and dreams: "I don't take the present seriously."

They stood in silent awe at the apprehension of works of literature that, in their minute evocation of the indescribable, meant that they would not need to write themselves.

Impact

things used to have an influence; now they have an impact
on managers or therapists or journalists

this is how a language dies
the crushing awareness of futility

the impact of words on reality
like breath on a window

Television

V: they should have quit when they were behind;
the desperate cry for help across the cosmos;
the empty tomb

better that than a limping mini-series
guess which supporting actor desperate for a career
will get killed-off this week

whoever created Coronation Street must have seen A Taste of Honey
and missed the point
it is not about kitchen sinks; it's about dream
the penultimate and best episode of The Prisoner begins
– Who is Number One?
– YOU are, Number Six

Arrival's hand-me-down orwellianisms had long since given way
to a witty dissection of conformity and rebellion
which turn out to be synonyms

I do not eat scorpions

I do not eat scorpions, no matter how many compliments my long black coat trails in its wake. I remain faithful to the oppressive years, the unexcavated language. The night, an ugly old feminist no one invited, intruded sharply; the winds blowing in from a cold unpolluted century sting us into awareness. The city's classical façades are ergomaniacal; they despise our decadence, our anonymity, and would stifle us in dialects and forms. I slipped in dog shit and my coat is in tatters.

Axis Mundi

I tried to import the words from
a shared book balanced nervously

myths to which we lack the references

seeker of a soft voice that
stabs you in the stomach

chained to desks in the muffled twilight
a random encounter interrupts the scenario's bleakness

gladly unofficial despots annihilate your experiences
and force you into writing essays

"you haven't really brought out the
indescribable horror"
how could I
if it's indescribable?

dusk admits the losers, the loving and the dead
and Friday night's legends stumble off to bed

A Portrait of the Piss-Artist as a Young Conservative

One October evening, my residence was infiltrated by two kinky spies. They came as a welcome relief from the French teachers, mechanics and JobCentrePlus employees whose ambitions seemed to consist of dragging me down and preventing me from thinking. The first spy was dressed in a black leather catsuit; she had insinuated herself into the ebon-draped master bedroom shortly before the final pavane. Sorry: I forgot to mention there was a ball going on downstairs.

"And what do you do here?" she inquired, giving me a sardonic smile.

"You could describe me as a mauvais-viveur," I replied.

She nodded thoughtfully and the tips of her dark hair brushed against the shiny studs of her dog collar. "Aren't you concerned about being thought a weirdo?"

"I'm not just a weirdo," I crowed. "I am the weirdest person you ever will meet."

It reminded me of the old days when I had been employed – on a temporary basis – as a beggar on the dusty multinational streets of Babylon. Crouched at the paw of a colossal winged lion representing Kakka, Lord of Images, I found myself accosted by a palace guard.

"You have been seated here for two hours," he observed, "and have barely earned a farthing of a shekel. Either you are the most inept mendicant in the Empire, or a secret agent."

"You only said that to practise the stative," I rejoined.

But I'm getting ahead of (or behind) myself. The spy in the bedroom was not happy; in fact she was downright peeved.

"I think of life as straightforward," she said, "and I find it hard to understand people who feel otherwise."

"Congratulations," I responded. "It looks like you've got all the cards. You can go and play solitaire."

Flashing me a furious glance, she pulled the rug from under my feet and in the vertiginous fall that ensued my vision encompassed her surprised stare; the dark window framing a sky like a fabulous city, crumbling and half-remembered.

I came to in the tower room of my Victorian abode, a venerable country mansion called Inner-City Slum.

Trees.

That night I went out to a goth club, where I saw the second kinky spy, but she was otherwise engaged. Cocaine streaked my memories like chrome lines in a metropolitan dawn.

I slept in. More trees. Sunny nihilism of 1989 summer; a portrait of the piss-artist as a Young Conservative. In a child's bedroom, surrounded by broken models, I scribbled to correct the past. Rain was forecast across the country – on our great adventure it starred the lights of passing cars – buffeting damp the grey stone of morning school.

One sharp wintry night, the second spy joined me on the edge and we talked about secrets yet to be encoded.

"You have to be careful when you walk down these streets, not to appear too weak or threatening, to give off no sexual or malodorous signs, nor to place your faith in foreign languages or religions."

"Why? Is this a place of existence-shattering beauty, the all-encompassing tolerance of love, when but to trace the curve of a bus's turn is a vital and impossible battle in stylistics? No, I didn't think so."

It was then that we entered the mythical 1980s, not to be confused with the real decade of a similar name. In this Nineteen Eighty Dash, almost everyone was unemployed and spoke Scouse, except for a small clique of New Romantics who would challenge silk-suited Floridian detectives to Sinclair C5 races through the orange-strobed night.

The two kinky spies were both escapees from the mythical 1960s, so did not look too out-of-place; although it was disconcerting to see them change towards the end of the evening from monochrome into colour, put flowers in their hair and start lurking around Carnaby Street for a love-in to infiltrate.

I passed the dark ruins of a sugar factory, jutting a denunciatory finger at the murky sunset, reduced in its rubble to a subject for photography students, harassed for spare cash and suicides.

The two kinky spies were aiding the police with their investigation into a serial killer who had graduated from an unhealthy obsession with Edgar Allan Poe to an emulation of Clark Ashton Smith. He would leave the police florid messages infused with recondite words which they had to go and look up in a dictionary. The kinky spies concluded that he was more interested in language than violence.

They had also been involved in finding a bomb that had been planted in a school and designed to detonate as soon as a teacher said something patronising or irrelevant. As the school hall filled desultorily for Monday morning assembly and the deputy Head approached the lectern, the two kinky spies rushed in shouting "No!"

Vienna in the snow. Or possibly Prague.

We were engrossed in the study of dead artists. (I have never told you, but I have made a study of these forbidden subjects.)

Fräulein Vergessenheit was suspected of dealing in secrets. We ended up following her to a black-and-white cinema show at the old Imperial Residenz, exchanging nervous glances throughout the artful presentation. We then wended our way back through the chiaroscuro city to the Pension Mitternacht: it was cold, but at least home for a while. People affected indifference to our pasts.

Far below, an old man unlocked the door to a quiet apartment where I wish we lived.

We were awakened by the reappearance of someone we had not seen in several years. We had been haunted by her absence, her insightful texts late at night, her lightning telegrams.

It seemed that all these empty romantic interludes had been designed to divert me from my real mission, and to make life more bearable. A little lust and we started acting like characters in a Russian novel.

Then out of the blue, the first kinky spy sent me a message that she was leaving the country. We arranged a clandestine meeting on the Pont Neuf which, for the purpose of our story, crosses the Vltava River connecting East and West Berlin. The Wall had come down; or maybe it hadn't been put up yet.

"I'm not lying," she insisted.

"I didn't think you were lying; I was thinking you were incomprehensible."

We discussed King Canute's plans to invade England: we sincerely hoped that he would be too busy doing his A levels to bother.

At that moment, a superfluity of dominatrices passed over the bridge.

"Is it your function in life to upset me?" I asked the kinky spy.

"No," she smiled. "It's just a hobby."

I left her for the tavern on the bridge where adventurers would congregate before setting out on dangerous missions; they gave me an invitation to a voyage to Cythera, a violent Liverpool punk dream; I spent most of Easter at Chapter One striving to recreate the city; intoxication of nights and the threat of morning comedowns, irritations and explanations. I got turned into a caricature in someone else's novel.

Lot of Excellent titles from
London Poetry Books

Tiny Collisions.	Poppy Dillon
Dark Matter.	Amy Neilson Smith
Twisted and Chewed.	Shaun Rivers
Joy Fear and F—k It.	Ant Smith
Pathways.	Anne Gaelan
Sky-high Down to Ground.	Keith Robert Bray
The Mirrors of Thespis	Keith Robert Bray
Pocket Full of Whispers	Keith Robert Bray
English is a Foreign,	
Language.	Alain English
Outside in Musin on life,	
as an Autistic Poet.	Alain English
Swimming with Endorphins.	Fran Isherwood
Ooetry.	Wendy Young
Going with the Flow.	Habiba Hrida
Rhymes for the Times.	Habiba Hrida
Making it Verse.	Habiba Hrida
I'm not here for your,	
Entertainment.	Tara Fleur
Life and Hope.	Jason Harris
Death Suicide Despair Poetry.	Jason Harris
When London Finally gave,	
In and started to Love.	Ernie Burns
The Bird of Morning.	IDF. Andrew

All titles £12.00 each
discount code available
www.londonpoetrybooks.com